RAMIT

SETHI

BIOGRAPHY

How He Dreamed
Big and Got Rich.

MAURICE PENCE

Table of Contents

INTRODUCTION

In this book, we will delve into the life and work of Ramit Sethi, a renowned personal finance expert, accomplished business owner, and prolific writer hailing from the United States. Meet the mastermind behind the entrepreneur-focused website "I Will Teach You to Be Rich." This platform offers invaluable guidance on personal finance, careers, and business.

In the early days of his professional journey, he embarked on a career as a management consultant in the technology industry. However, as time went on, his interests shifted towards entrepreneurship and personal finance. In 2009, a remarkable book was released by Sethi titled "I Will Teach You to Be Rich". Its popularity soared, making it a bestseller in no time.

The author has since gone on to publish several more books, among them "Your Move: The Underdog's Guide to Building Your Business", "The Psychology of Money," and "The Ultimate Guide to Habits: Peak Performance Made Easy."

In recent years, there has been a great deal of public interest in the personal life of Ramit Sethi. In the following pages, we will explore the life and work of Ramit Sethi, delving into the details of his background, accomplishments, and philosophy. Join us on a journey of discovery as we seek to understand the man behind the name.

Chapter 1

WHO IS RAMIT SETHI?

From his modest origins, Ramit Sethi rose to the ranks of a successful entrepreneur and a renowned author with a best-selling book. While the counsel shared on his blog may not be revolutionary, it is his unique perspective that distinguishes him from others.

With an unwavering commitment to the truth, he fearlessly imparts the necessary wisdom for achieving success. If you have been let down by other financial experts, Sethi could be the one to turn to.

Early Life

On a sunny day in California, June 30, 1982, marked the arrival of Ramit Sethi into this world. Sethi's lineage traces back to two Indian immigrants who established Pavlok, a company specializing in wearable technology that facilitates the cessation of negative habits and the cultivation of positive ones.

Sethi's formative years were spent at Bella Vista High School in California, where he distinguished himself through his academic prowess and enthusiastic involvement in extracurricular pursuits.

Upon graduating from high school with outstanding achievements, Sethi embarked on a journey to pursue advanced education at Stanford University. During his time at Stanford University, Sethi pursued a degree in science, technology, and society with a minor in psychology.

During this period, a fascination with comprehending human behavior took hold of him, prompting him to pursue a higher education. He subsequently earned a Master's degree in sociology from the same institution.

Sethi's remarkable academic achievements and fervent interest in comprehending human behavioral tendencies, coupled with his financial management expertise, have made him a highly coveted authority in the realm of personal finance counseling in contemporary times.

According to Business Insider, Sethi's financial coaching programs have aided numerous individuals in launching their own businesses. In 2019, he released the second edition of his book, which features a 6-week program aimed at helping readers effectively manage their finances.

Moreover, he is the host of his own podcast, bearing the identical name, "I Will Teach You to Be Rich."

Early Career Interests

Over the course of the past decade, Ramit Sethi has amassed a significant following through his blog and online courses. The blending of candid and occasionally confrontational guidance with lightheartedness and amusement is especially valued by readers belonging to the Gen Y cohort.

Sethi was never one to sugarcoat the truth or shy away from potentially upsetting others with his honesty. His unique approach to personal finance sets him apart from numerous other experts in the field.

If you find yourself struggling to make headway in your financial situation despite your best efforts, I would recommend perusing Sethi's blog as a potential resource.

Ramit Sethi's Family

Maneesh Sethi is Ramit Sethi's younger brother. His parents, Neelam and Prab Sethi, are also in the picture.

Like his famous older sibling, Maneesh has made a name for himself in the business world as the creator and chief executive officer of the successful Pavlok watch company.

Pavlok is a wearable gadget that employs electrical stimulation to aid in the formation of healthy habits and the elimination of unhealthy ones.

Mrs. Sethi uprooted her life and emigrated to the United States in 1982. The year her firstborn son entered the world.

Chapter 2

PROFESSIONAL LIFE

Ramit's Career Journey

During his academic years, Ramit, a bright college student, developed a keen interest in personal finances. The genesis of his interest in this topic can be traced back to a challenging experience he encountered in his inaugural year at university.

Regrettably, he forfeited fifty percent of his scholarship funds as a result of unwise investment decisions on the stock exchange. The experience proved to be a turning point for him, as he came to the realization that the commonly touted wisdom on financial management was insufficient and failed to capture the full complexity of the subject matter.

Ramit embarked on a journey of self-discovery and personal growth, delving deeply into the world of personal finance through extensive reading and research.

In his time at Stanford, he made an effort to impart his knowledge on personal finance to his fellow students by conducting classes. However, he was met with silence and received no response from his peers at first.

However, the course of events shifted when he unveiled his website, "I Will Teach You to Be Rich," which garnered widespread recognition among individuals seeking pragmatic guidance on proficiently handling their finances.

Upon completing his studies, Ramit was presented with a remarkable opportunity to collaborate with none other than the esteemed marketing expert, Seth Godin.

Throughout this period, he refined his abilities in the field of marketing and acquired invaluable expertise by collaborating with distinguished professionals in the industry.

Upon concluding his internship with Seth Godin, Ramit embarked on co-founding PBWorks (formerly PBWiki), a non-profit entity dedicated to enhancing business collaboration through the utilization of wiki technology.

The Creation and Growth of His Personal Finance Blog

Ramit Sethi's childhood was marked by his reserved nature, a stark contrast to his current bold and flamboyant demeanor. As the time for college arrived, he was accepted into Stanford University. The sole impediment lay in the fact that his parents were unable to bear the cost of the tuition.

Nevertheless, Sethi remained undaunted. He was determined to cover his own expenses. In his book, Sethi recounts how he devised an efficient organizational system that enabled him to seamlessly apply for a whopping 60 scholarships.

His initial results weren't great, so he delved into what was going wrong and made improvements. As an illustration, he documented his interview preparation sessions and came to the realization that he was not displaying enough facial expressions.

As he strode confidently into his interviews, a grin played at the corners of his lips. Through his tireless efforts, he was able to reap the rewards of his labor. Sethi's remarkable academic achievements have earned them over $200,000 in scholarships.

His knowledge about money was limited. One of his first scholarship awards was a cash prize of $2,000, and he wisely put all of that money into a single stock. Sethi lost half of his money and learned the importance of diversifying his investments.

And so began his quest to unravel the mysteries of the financial world. Immersed in a world of literature, he devoured every book within his reach, unearthing startling themes along the way.

To his mind, much of the advice proffered by authorities lacked practicality. The pundits expounded their wisdom, yet the words fell on deaf ears as no one heeded their counsel.

Sethi's book recounts how he merged his expertise in psychology with his newfound financial acumen to launch a blog that imparted practical money wisdom to his readers.

The success of his blog, "I Will Teach You to Be Rich," eventually paved the way for the publication of his book with the same title. In addition, Ramit Sethi crafted a collection of digital courses aimed at assisting individuals with financial difficulties.

The Success of His Books and Business

Ramit Sethi, the founder of "I Will Teach You To Be Rich" and "GrowthLab," has established two successful businesses. "I Will Teach You to Be Rich" is a book that chronicles the author's personal journey towards achieving financial success.

Through clear and concise step-by-step instructions, readers are able to follow along and learn how to improve their own financial situations.

Aspiring entrepreneurs seeking to establish and expand their online businesses can turn to

"GrowthLab," a business accelerator that provides comprehensive support and guidance to achieve success. In addition to his blog, he generates revenue through book sales and email marketing.

Ramit's success in earning money from his blogs can inspire you to start your own and generate a respectable online income with minimal effort. Ramit's YouTube channel, "I will teach you to be rich," boasts over 200K subscribers.

Ramit Sethi Podcast

The Ramit Sethi Show is a captivating podcast that delves into a plethora of subjects pertaining to personal finance on a weekly basis. Ramit conducts interviews with a diverse range of individuals, spanning various professions such as entrepreneurship, business ownership, and financial expertise.

Ramit's listeners are presented with lucid and practical guidance that can be implemented to enhance their financial situation.

His Online Courses

Ramit, a triumphant entrepreneur and author, provides online courses on various topics such as personal finance, freelancing, productivity, and more.

Ramit is a renowned financial expert who has empowered countless individuals to attain their financial aspirations through his literary works, educational programs, and various other avenues.

Through his unwavering commitment, he has garnered great admiration from his global supporters, resulting in substantial wealth and acclaim as one of the foremost figures on the planet.

Chapter 3

PHILOSOPHY AND TEACHINGS

His Approach to Personal Finance and Growth

Ramit Sethi's financial advice is straightforward and commonly echoed by other experts in the field. What separates Sethi from the competition is his methodology. As he embarked on his blogging journey, his focus centered on the realm of education.

He pondered that perhaps individuals were not adhering to a budget due to a lack of knowledge on the subject. Most financial experts tend to follow this approach. Sethi discovered that a multitude of individuals possessed knowledge regarding topics such as budgeting. They failed to accomplish it.

He redirected his attention from imparting knowledge to delving into the underlying motivations behind individuals' financial behaviors. The author suggests making

19

incremental adjustments to enhance crucial aspects of your life rather than implementing drastic modifications.

Ramit Sethi's reputation precedes him for his straightforwardness. He endeavors to avoid pandering to his readers by refraining from simply exhorting them to believe that they possess the capacity to accomplish anything they conceive in their minds.

He candidly expresses his viewpoints, interweaving lightheartedness and humor. With his frank yet exaggerated approach, he has garnered a significant following among readers of Generation Y.

The Role of Thought and Behavior in Financial Success

Automating your finances is a fundamental principle in Sethi's philosophy. Implement an automated system for your credit card payments to avoid any concerns regarding delayed payments.

Implement an automated investment strategy to eliminate the need for manual transfers of funds into your 401(k) account. By automating all tasks, you can optimize your cognitive abilities and resources for other important matters.

Post-automation, Sethi's recommendations can be summarized into four key financial principles: initiate investments at the earliest opportunity, allocate funds for future expenses, reduce expenses on non-essential items, and uphold a favorable credit score.

According to Sethi, implementing these four strategies can give you a competitive edge over 99% of individuals. Sethi suggests beginning investments at an early age when it comes to financial planning. Making investments at a young age can lead to substantial wealth creation, even with a limited initial investment.

Diversifying your investment portfolio with low-cost ETFs is a sound financial strategy. Investing in individual stocks can be challenging for novice investors. One should avoid investing a significant amount of money and incurring substantial losses, similar to Sethi's experience during his initial investment phase.

Diversifying your financial objectives is recommended, and investing should not be the sole focus. It is advisable to allocate funds for your future financial needs.

Establish a contingency fund to safeguard your financial well-being. Initiate saving funds for significant future expenses such as a matrimonial ceremony, the initial payment for a property, or a holiday trip.

Insufficient savings? Explore additional sources of income. Increasing one's income is the key to achieving greater savings, despite the additional effort required. You can improve your financial situation by reducing expenses on non-essential items.

Sethi is of the opinion that saving cannot be achieved solely through frugality. Individuals who prioritize their efforts towards minimizing expenses fail to recognize the larger financial perspective. It is advisable to allocate funds toward your priorities while refraining from unnecessary expenses.

Review your expenses and identify areas where you are incurring unwanted expenditures. Are you currently paying for a magazine subscription that is no longer being utilized?

Are you effectively utilizing the entirety of your monthly paid phone data? Is a weekly expenditure of $100 on socializing with friends, despite not deriving pleasure from it, a sound financial decision?

The ultimate objective is to have a clear understanding of your expenses. Then you can allocate your funds towards the expenses that hold value to you. Maintaining a good credit score is a prudent financial strategy for long-term savings.

Ensure that you settle all your bills completely and avoid carrying any outstanding balances. A 0% balance transfer could potentially result in cost savings for individuals with outstanding credit card debt.

However, it is not advisable to solely focus on balance transfers without making full payments to clear the outstanding balance. It is advisable to optimize the benefits of your credit cards. Select a credit card that offers rewards based on your spending habits.

His Advice and Tips for Building Wealth and Living A Rich Life

For those who are prepared to embark on an investment journey but are uncertain about the initial steps, seeking guidance from a financial advisor may be a prudent choice. Discovering a suitable financial advisor need not be a daunting task.

With SmartAsset's complimentary service, you will be paired with as many as three trusted financial advisors who operate in your locality.

You will have the opportunity to conduct interviews with your recommended advisors at no charge, allowing you to determine which one is the best fit for your needs.

Should you be prepared to embark on a journey towards discovering a financial advisor who can assist you in realizing your aspirations, commence your search without delay. Having a commendable credit score can prove to be highly advantageous in the long haul.

Raising one's loan approval odds is an aim worth pursuing. Qualifying for credit cards with higher rewards can be advantageous. A lofty credit score can also aid in achieving aspirations, such as acquiring that ideal abode.

Raising one's credit score can be achieved through the implementation of straightforward measures. Paying your bills in full each month is a significant step towards financial stability.

In the pursuit of a better credit score, one may adopt various financial habits. Here are a few such practices that can potentially enhance your creditworthiness:

For those with less than stellar credit histories, there is hope for improvement through diligent effort. Improving your credit score is a top priority, and you are committed to making progress every day, week, month, and year.

Chapter 4

BUSINESS PHILOSOPHY AND APPROACH

Budgets Being Pointless.

Would you like to discover how to increase your savings? As advised by numerous financial experts, the recommended course of action is to devise a budget and curtail your expenditures. Ramit Sethi, the personal finance coach, asserts that budgets are not effective for the majority of individuals.

In the revised edition of his book, "I Will Teach You to be Rich," Sethi remarks that the advice of personal finance experts to "establish a budget!" is the type of unhelpful recommendation that may make them feel good, but it fails to engage the average reader, who may find the topic tedious.

Why Budgets Don't Typically Work

If we were instructed to cease spending and commence saving, the majority of individuals would likely be uncertain of how to proceed. Tracking every single daily purchase can be a daunting task, and even with a budget in place, it may not always deter one from spending.

"Budgets are a waste of time since they just serve to make us feel horrible about ourselves without offering any useful insight into the future," says Sethi.

According to Sethi, budgets only exacerbate these negative emotions without offering any helpful guidance for the future. They seem to serve no purpose at all. Sethi's frustration was shared by many.

The same thing was said by Chris Reining, who left his IT career at age 37 with almost $1 million saved, to CNBC Make It. Budgets don't work, Reining says on his blog. "The main reason I don't think they work is that people can't keep to them," he said.

In his musings, he likened the act of budgeting to that of following a poor diet. Do you know anyone who is constantly experimenting with various diets but never seems to achieve the desired results?

Here's What to Do Instead:

Ramit Sethi proposes a different approach to financial planning than creating a budget, which requires reflecting on past expenditures and making adjustments. His term for this is "conscious spending."

The first stage is to allocate your income to cover your fixed expenses, your investments, your savings objectives, and any discretionary spending you want to do.

According to Sethi's recommendations, fixed expenditures (such as rent, food, and school loans) may eat up to 50–60% of your income.

Savings for long-term objectives like a trip or a down payment on a house should make up 5–10% of your total savings, while investments like your 401(k), Roth IRA, and taxable investing accounts should make up the remaining 5–10%.

The remaining 20%–35% of your budget may be freely spent however you choose. By prioritizing payments like this, you can be certain that your financial obligations will be met.

The surplus might then be used for necessities and savings. If you've already budgeted for your rent, food, and transportation, then you may purchase anything you want from the "guilt-free spending" category.

Stop worrying about where your money goes each month, Sethi advises. He isn't advocating wasteful spending on the sly. Instead, this method will save you the stress of deciding whether or not to get a latte on the way to work every day.

Spend lavishly on what matters most to you and ruthlessly slash expenses elsewhere, he suggests. Instead of keeping a tight rein on every cent you spend, choose an item—like a vacation—that you're eager to put money toward.

If you follow Sethi's plan, you won't have to worry about pinpointing where you can make cuts to save $100 every month or $1200 per year.

Instead, just take $100 out of your discretionary budget per month. You may save without even thinking about it if you set up recurring transfers from your checking account into a savings account.

The best part is that you won't feel pressured to save for a vacation you'll never take. The same can be said for your money, your investments, and every other aspect of your life if you switch your spending habits from a retrospective to a prospective stance.

Don't beat yourself up about your inability to stick to a budget. Almost no one sticks to his or her financial plan. Rather than asking, "What do I want my money to do for me?" you may wish to ask, "Where do I want my money to go?"

Chapter 5

PERSONAL DEVELOPMENT TIPS

Where to Put Your Money

O ver the course of time, investing your funds can prove to be a fruitful method of expanding your financial assets. Should one hastily open a brokerage account? Perhaps in due time.

According to Ramit Sethi, a personal finance expert and entrepreneur, there are other accounts that are worth saving and investing in prior to opening a brokerage account.

The following is his recommended hierarchy for saving and investing, which he deems wise to adhere to:

Contribute to A 401(K) Plan to Get Your Employer's Match.

Unfortunately, 401(k) plans are not offered by every company. However, if your company offers a 401(k) plan with a matching contribution

33

component, it is in your best interest to contribute at least enough to get the entire match.

There is no universally accepted ratio since it is up to the discretion of each organization. Workers under the age of 50 may now put away up to $19,500 annually into a 401(k), while those 50 and over can put away up to $26,000.

In most cases, businesses won't even get close to such limits. However, if your company would match your contributions up to a certain amount — say, $3,000 — then it is in your best interest to contribute at least that much.

Contribute to A Roth IRA

One of the most remarkable features of Roth IRAs is the perpetual exemption from taxes on investment gains within the account and the ability to withdraw funds during retirement without incurring any tax liability.

As of now, the yearly maximum amount that one can contribute to a Roth IRA is $6,000 for individuals under the age of 50 and $7,000 for those who are 50 years old or older. As Roth IRAs are self-funded, one would not be eligible for a company match, unlike a 401(k).

Max Out Your 401(K).

Most workers in the middle income bracket cannot contribute the maximum to the 401(k) plan. If you've already contributed the maximum to a Roth IRA and still have money left over for savings and investments, you'd be wise to deposit that money into a 401(k).

The IRS will tax you less on your salary if you contribute more to your traditional 401(k). Unfortunately, this isn't a perk you get with a Roth IRA, so don't expect any quick tax savings if you decide to open one.

However, for those who expect to be in a higher tax band in retirement than they are now, Roth IRAs are a great option since investment profits and withdrawals are tax-free.

Max Out Your Health Savings Account.

Health savings accounts (HSAs) are not open to everyone. A high-deductible health insurance plan is required for participation. Plans with deductibles of $1,400 or more for individual coverage or $2,800 or more for family coverage meet this criteria for the current calendar year.

Health savings accounts (HSAs) combine the best features of a Roth IRA with those of a standard 401(k). Contributions to an HSA are deducted before taxes, and any funds not needed for emergency medical treatment may be invested tax-free.

As long as the funds are utilized to pay for eligible medical expenditures, both investment gains and withdrawals from an HSA are exempt from federal income tax.

The money you put into an HSA during your working years may be used for healthcare expenses in retirement at any time. You may also take advantage of tax-deferred investment opportunities.

The current HSA contribution limits for those under the age of 55 are $3,850 per year for self-only coverage and $7,750 per year for family coverage.

These amounts increase to $4,600 and $8,200, respectively, if you are 55 or older.

Put Your Money in A Regular Bank Account.

After exhausting the aforementioned accounts, it may be prudent to contemplate investing any surplus funds in a conventional brokerage account. In the realm of personal finance, it is widely acknowledged that conventional brokerage accounts do not provide any tax advantages.

Therefore, it is advisable to prioritize the utilization of accounts that do offer tax breaks before considering traditional brokerage accounts.

Brokerage accounts, on the other hand, offer a greater degree of flexibility. In the realm of retirement savings, it is customary that a withdrawal from a 401(k) account prior to reaching the age of 59 would result in a penalty.

The flexibility of Roth IRAs notwithstanding, there exist certain regulations that must be adhered to in order to access your funds prior to reaching the age of 5912.

You will be fined if you use your HSA money for something other than medical expenses. The money you put into a brokerage account is yours to withdraw at any time, no questions asked.

Chapter 6

RAMIT SETHI'S 10 MONEY RULES

Key Points

Maintaining a set of financial guidelines is crucial for ensuring sound management of one's finances. Sethi's foremost focus lies in leading a fulfilling life and investing in items that enhance his overall well-being and bring him joy.

Allowing your finances to run unchecked is among the most detrimental actions you can take. Do even the affluent, or perhaps particularly the affluent, adhere to financial guidelines?

Ramit Sethi, the renowned personal finance expert, comes to mind. Within the pages of his book, he shares a collection of ten invaluable money rules that have proven to be instrumental in keeping his finances on track. Let us examine them and the rationale behind them.

Have A One-Year Emergency Fund.

Having an emergency fund readily available can prove to be a lifesaver in times of unforeseen financial obligations. The question of how much one should have on hand is a common one.

For a considerable period, the majority of experts advocated for a six-month reserve fund. The course of events took a turn following the tumultuous financial upheaval caused by the COVID-19 pandemic.

As an illustration, Suze Orman has amended her counsel from a six-month reserve to a minimum of eight months, with a year being preferable.

Sethi's perspective has undergone a recent shift, as he now advocates for a more robust emergency fund, increasing his recommended timeframe from six months to a full year.

It is commonly agreed upon that an emergency fund should be kept in the form of cash rather than being invested. In times of unforeseen circumstances, it is advisable to opt for a high-yield savings account that does not entail a plethora of requirements to fulfill.

Save 10%, Invest 20%.

According to Sethi, it is recommended by most experts to save and invest a portion of your income, but he provides specific numerical values for this practice.

The author's personal finance strategy involves setting aside 10% of the gross income for savings and allocating 20% towards investments.

In the realm of personal finance, the allocation of a portion of one's income to savings is typically reserved for objectives of a more immediate nature.

Among the financial goals that one may set are those that pertain to the creation of an emergency fund, the financing of a summer vacation, the establishment of a new-car fund, or the accumulation of funds for a house down payment.

The investing segment pertains to tangible investments, such as your retirement account. Throughout your personal experience, you need to realize that investing in the stock market has been a more lucrative option compared to the returns obtained from a savings account.

This has been a well-established fact throughout history. According to Sethi's perspective, while savings may aid in daily expenses, it is investments that pave the way to wealth.

Have the Cash for Large Expenses.

One should refrain from making large purchases if they do not have the necessary funds readily available. Sethi advises that one should always have the financial means to afford any desired indulgence, be it a luxurious getaway or a brand new automobile.

Paying in cash is not the only option; Sethi is a well-known advocate of credit card rewards. You can learn the importance of avoiding debt when making purchases. It's best to have the funds readily available to pay off the purchase immediately rather than take on debt.

He did concede that purchasing a house outright with cash may not always be a practical option, acknowledging some flexibility in the matter of housing. Nevertheless, should you lack a minimum of a 20% down payment, you are not yet prepared.

Don't Question Every Purchase.

Ramit Sethi's central message revolves around the idea that each of us should strive to lead a fulfilling and prosperous life. It is imperative to identify the small indulgences that bring us immense pleasure and unhesitatingly indulge in them.

Sethi's book encompasses a diverse range of interests, from literature to wellness, culinary delights, and philanthropy. Among the highlights are his passion for reading, his commitment to maintaining good health, his love of savory starters, and his generosity in supporting a friend's charitable cause. He spends money on everything listed without agonizing over the cost.

In essence, refrain from scrutinizing the minor acquisitions that bring you joy and simply indulge in them.

Fly Business Class on Long Flights.

For flights longer than four hours, Ramit Sethi always books business class (or first class when traveling domestically). In addition, everyone recognizes this as a standard operating procedure.

Business class is not only more luxurious but also offers additional benefits that may make the upgrade worthwhile. Pre-flight lounge access is virtually priceless, as are the complimentary food and beverages, checked luggage, and other perks.

Put Money Towards Quality Over Quantity.

We wholeheartedly endorse another one of Sethi's rules. In our experience, it's always been wise to invest in the highest-quality version of a product and make the most of it for as long as feasible.

Investing in a high-quality item can prove to be a wise decision, as it can withstand the test of time and outlast its cheaper counterparts by several decades.

This not only saves you money in the long run but also spares you the hassle of having to replace it frequently. Using it will provide you with an enhanced experience.

We shall, however, impose our own caveat on this rule: one should exercise caution and consider whether the item is truly necessary before making an investment in it.

When embarking on a new hobby, it is wise to begin with inexpensive equipment or supplies. Once you have determined that you are committed to the pursuit, you can then consider upgrading to higher-quality materials.

Don't Cap Spending on Health.

It is a melancholic truth that we are bestowed with only one physical vessel. It is imperative that one take care of it. According to Sethi's philosophy, one should not limit the expenditure on health-related expenses, be it a premium gym membership or high-quality food.

And indeed, your mental health is also encompassed within this category!

Work with People You Respect.

Sethi muses that a delightful aspect of achieving financial independence is the liberation from interacting with individuals who fail to meet one's standards of likability or respectability.

One can make the decision to terminate, recruit, or resign as necessary in order to reach a point where all colleagues are deserving of their time and consideration.

Achieving the financial position that Sethi currently enjoys, which affords him the ability to make such decisions, may require a considerable amount of time for many of us.

Live Outside the Spreadsheet.

After setting up your personal finance spreadsheets, automating your savings, and gaining control over your finances, it's time to live your life to the fullest.

Make it a priority to spend quality time with your loved ones, cherished friends, and engaging hobbies. For what other reason are you engaging in all of this?

Marry the Right Person.

As you embark on the journey of life, your spouse will be your steadfast companion, sharing not only your joys and sorrows but also your financial responsibilities.

The issue of financial incompatibility has been known to be a leading cause of marital dissolution. It is imperative to engage in several discussions regarding your financial values well in advance of your wedding day.

Chapter 7

10 BRILLIANT LESSONS FROM RAMIT'S SUCCESS

Ramit Sethi's net worth exceeds $25 million. The bulk of his riches stem from his various online ventures, such as "I Will Teach You To Be Rich," Growth Lab, and exclusive web-based courses.

In 2004, Ramit embarked on his blogging journey while pursuing his studies in technology and psychology at Stanford. He embarked on his online journey by selling a $4.95 eBook.

Ramit's online businesses generate millions of dollars in revenue annually. One may wonder how he managed to transform from nothing to establishing a business worth millions.

In the following pages, we shall delve into Ramit Sethi's net worth and the valuable insights we can glean from his triumphant online endeavors.

Lesson 1: Develop "Systems", Not Goals.

Ramit Sethi's reputation precedes him as a master of creating and refining systems that streamline and automate a wide range of tasks.

He opined that constructing systems is a challenging endeavor, but the rewards can be reaped for a period of two decades or more. For those who may be interested, here is a selection of the systems Sethi has crafted throughout his years of experience:

In his book, Ramit shares insights on various topics such as finances, automatic saving and investing, working with his assistant to save over 20 hours per week, his experience with the scholarship system, which helped him apply for over 65 college scholarships, and his daily productivity strategies.

The aforementioned systems have played a pivotal role in Ramit Sethi's net worth exceeding 25 million dollars. Before embarking on the construction of a system, it is imperative that you determine the desired outcome.

As you strive towards your desired outcome, it is imperative to select a singular focus that will propel you forward. Consistently refining your approach to this chosen pursuit will yield remarkable results.

For those who may still be pondering the distinction between systems and goals, allow Sethi to provide a straightforward illustration:

As an entrepreneur, your aspiration may be to establish a business worth a million dollars. The system you employ serves as the foundation for testing product ideas, recruiting the ideal team, and drawing in lucrative clients.

It's not unheard of for bloggers to aim for a monthly income of $10,000 via their writing. In order to make money, you need an audience, which your system develops a content plan for.

Is that what you mean? Everything about the system is flawless.

Lesson 2: Start Small, Grow Big.

Ramit was once asked on Twitter by someone, "What if I desire to have an 8-figure business?" In his response, he stated that the unvarnished reality is that the majority of individuals prefer to fantasize about managing a business worth a million dollars rather than operating a business worth only $10,000.

And thus, they found themselves at a crossroads where the pursuit of their aspirations appeared to be an insurmountable challenge, leading them to a state of inaction. Thus, it became apparent to him that beginning with modest steps was crucial.

Sethi reflects on the notion that every accomplished person was once a novice. As you look back on your own journey, be reminded that even the most successful professionals started out as amateurs.

This realization will give you hope and motivation to pursue your own passions, knowing that with dedication and hard work, you too can achieve greatness.

Through perseverance and dedication, Sethi was able to develop his skills and knowledge to become an expert in his field. This insight has taught him to approach new endeavors with humility and a willingness to learn, knowing that even the most accomplished individuals have to start somewhere.

Even Ramit Sethi does not constitute an exception in this regard. He embarked on his online journey by selling a humble $4.95 ebook. He now presides over a thriving multimillion-dollar enterprise. Let your aspirations soar and commence at this very moment!

Lesson 3: Earn Money on The Side.

For those who are employed in a traditional 9-to-5 job, it may be beneficial to explore additional avenues for generating income. Consider embarking on a side hustle.

A side hustle can be a valuable means of generating income beyond the confines of a traditional 9-to-5 job. The prospect of earning more money can grant you the liberty to chase your aspirations.

Ramit's journey to building a million-dollar business online was fueled by his relentless pursuit of side hustles. He explored various avenues, such as starting a blog, offering services, selling books, and more, all in a bid to earn money online.

Lesson 4: Focus on Action, Not Consumption.

One may peruse an abundance of blogs and email newsletters to their heart's content. Without taking action, life remains stagnant and changeless.

Many individuals tend to wait for events to unfold instead of taking action to create them. Such is the reason why the majority of individuals lead commonplace lives.

Ramit Sethi is the kind of guy who gets things done. As soon as an idea strikes him, he promptly sets it into motion. A pivotal factor contributing to his immense triumph is his adeptness at expeditiously transforming concepts into action.

Lesson 5: Create Premium Courses That Offer Huge Value.

Ramit's blog offers the vast majority of its content free of charge, with a mere 2% of its material requiring payment. Only a mere 2% of his vast knowledge is accessible through his free resources, while the remaining wealth of information can be unlocked through his exclusive premium online courses. To date, he has authored over 20 thriving online products.

The spectrum of prices spans from a modest $100 to a staggering $25,000. Ramit and his team dedicate a significant amount of time and financial resources to the development of their products.

The endeavor demands a great deal of diligent effort. Their diligent efforts bear fruit, as their courses are in high demand and sell like hotcakes right after their launch.

If you were to provide a complimentary offering, it may not necessarily resonate with your audience or clientele. In such a scenario, the audience's lack of interest remains unchanged.

It is imperative to take heed of the desires of your intended readership. Discovering their struggles and aspirations. The task at hand is to devise a solution and provide it in the form of a commodity or amenity. Following this strategy will bring about the results you want.

Lesson 6: Understand the Psychology of Money

Ramit has a well-known saying that goes, "Avoid inquiring about the $3 questions." Pose the inquiries worth $30,000. Agreed, his statement is correct.

Our preoccupation with scrimping and the accompanying remorse over indulging in a $5 cup of coffee often distracts us from a crucial inquiry: "What is the extent of our expenditure on investment fees?"

For numerous individuals, such a sum amounts to tens of thousands of dollars. Have you ever contemplated the art of negotiating your salary, which, over the course of your lifetime, may amount to a substantial sum exceeding $100,000?

Ramit's message is clear: in the pursuit of financial success, there is a finite limit to how much you can reduce your expenses. However, the potential for earning is boundless and limitless.

The Following Are Examples of Some Important Critical Factors:

- Preemptive spending,

56

- Continually and mechanically investing,

- Understanding investor psychology,

- salary negotiation techniques, and

- Organizing one's debt all falls under the category of "money skills."

However, a common grievance among individuals pertains to the increase in taxes and monthly subscription fees for services such as Netflix. The focus seems to be diverted from the significant aspects of life.

That's why it's so important to comprehend the mind behind the coin. Consider many options that might lead to an increase in your revenue. You should splurge on the things you value most and ruthlessly cut down on the rest. Ramit asserts that this is really the situation.

Check out Ramit's book if you're interested in learning about the psychology of money and the automated money method he employs.

Here is Ramit Sethi's advice on how to spend less than an hour each month on your finances if you're interested in learning how to manage your money properly.

Spend 30 minutes reviewing your finances every month, automate bill paying, saving, and investing, and concentrate on only one or two variable expenses (the rest are generally quite stable).

Lesson 7: Network with Influencers

Ramit's remarkable achievements can be attributed, in part, to his association with influential figures such as Tim Ferriss. Ramit Sethi's rapidly growing net worth can be attributed to this very reason.

He chronicles his encounters with nearly every influencer in the marketing industry through a series of interviews. When you establish strong connections with the key individuals in your industry, what are the resulting outcomes?

You would attain outcomes at a quicker pace. Networking holds immense significance, and that is precisely why it cannot be overlooked.

Lesson 8: Never Fast-Forward Your Way to Success.

The road to achievement is often paved with difficulties. The adage that all good things come to those who wait holds true in life.

From experience, we have found that many individuals struggle to generate income through online means due to the tendency to seek out quick and easy solutions.

In their pursuit of wealth, they seek out expedient solutions and are frequently ensnared by deceitful ploys. Make a conscious effort to steer clear of them, no matter what it takes.

One would benefit from seeking out a knowledgeable mentor or guide. You must possess a clear vision. You must discern your desires in both the personal and professional realms.

Please specify a time frame for completion, measured in years. In order to achieve your vision or goal, it is important to break it down into smaller, actionable tasks that can be accomplished within a few months. This is the winning formula!

Lesson 9: Take Part in The Online Community.

Ramit's daily routine involves spending a considerable amount of time browsing through various social media platforms such as Twitter, Instagram, Facebook, and YouTube.

Engaging with his "target audience" through social media is one of his regular activities. The utilization of social media platforms serves a multitude of purposes for him, which include:

1. To think of something fresh,

2. Build your social circle,

3. Talk about his insight,

4. Spread the word about his publications and more.

Aspiring to become an influencer or guru in your niche? Consider seeking out a platform or social media outlet that allows for consistent engagement with your followers.

Lesson 10: Build A Great Team.

Ramit's personnel play a critical role in his accomplishments. I Will Teach You to Be Rich and GrowthLab are two of his thriving web ventures.

If you're wondering what IWT is about, it's all about money and becoming your own boss. However, GrowthLab is focused on the online world. The other thing is that he produces a lot of stuff for each of them.

His output also includes video and audio podcasts. What's his secret, then? He is backed by a great crew that assists him in almost every aspect of his life.

Ideas for Discussion Topics, In a response to his email, Making something up, handling search engine optimization and social media promotion, product development, and sales And that's not all!

What's even better? When it comes to hiring, Ramit is tops. The majority of his workforce has experience working for either a Fortune 100 company or a venture capital-backed technology startup.

Chapter 8

IMPACT AND INFLUENCE

Top 3 'Toxic' Money Myths to Ditch

Maintaining financial stability and accumulating wealth can be quite challenging endeavors. You must avoid self-sabotage in order to prevent unnecessary difficulties.

Ramit Sethi, a successful entrepreneur and financial expert, recommends that overcoming personal obstacles is crucial to attaining financial goals. This advice is highlighted in his appearance on the Netflix series "How to Get Rich."

According to him, shedding three detrimental money beliefs can pave the way for a stable financial future, as reported by CNBC Make It. According to him, a mere shift in your investment mindset has the potential to transform your life significantly.

Within your thought process, there exist three indicators that may be impeding your progress:

Toxic Mindset No. 1:

The Topic of Money Is Off-Limits.

Sethi asserts that despite the cultural tendency among Americans to shy away from discussions concerning finances, such conversations are imperative for achieving success.

He pondered, "One cannot possibly progress without discussing finances, whether alone or with a companion." In any household that strives for financial success, the topic of money is a common and recurring theme.

To truly take charge of your financial situation, it is imperative to have a comprehensive understanding of your income, expenses, and aspirations for long-term financial stability. Without this clarity, it is impossible to take proactive steps towards achieving your financial goals.

According to Sethi, incorporating periodic self-reflection into your financial routine is a crucial aspect of cultivating a positive and sustainable rapport with money. My dear reader, I humbly inquire as to your thoughts on this matter.

What is the correct procedure to follow in order to do this task? Would you happen to be interested in this matter? Uncertainty lingers within us as to whether our current savings account is the optimal choice. Let us engage in a discussion.

Toxic Mindset No. 2:

Not Questioning Your Financial Upbringing

What we learn as children shapes our perspectives on money and how we use it throughout our lives. The incorrect route may be chosen if you refuse to challenge your teachings.

On his show, he'll ask married people, 'What did your parents ever tell you about money?' "We can't afford it" is one of the most frequent complaints he hears from families, according to Sethi. Consider the consequences of hearing it from your loved ones ten times in a row. In the thousands! 10,000 times.

When it comes to managing your money as an adult, the "invisible script" you developed as a child might come back to haunt you, says Sethi.

In this scenario, it might make you feel bad about treating yourself to a cup of coffee, despite the fact that you can afford it and are diligently putting money away for the future.

You may reset your mind by writing down the scripts from your youth. In financial terms, it can be stated as follows: One must recognize their financial goals, evaluate them thoroughly, and then determine which investment strategies to pursue or develop for the upcoming financial period.

Toxic Mindset No. 3:

People Without Money Don't Invest.

Perhaps you have the misconception that only the rich should consider investing. Sethi holds the belief that perspective is reversed. The act of making investments is the optimal method for accumulating a substantial amount of wealth.

You should invest as much of your first salary as you can. He said, "Even if you can only invest $20 a month, that's how you get started."

Set up direct deposits from your paycheck to your investing account so you don't have to think about it again until payday.

He states that through automated investing, one can potentially change their entire socioeconomic path for themselves and their family.

That's fantastic news because it means you can stop stressing about money and start enjoying life to the fullest right now and for the next two decades. That's because your money is working hard for you at a compounding rate while you're busy enjoying your life.

The process of accumulating substantial wealth requires a considerable amount of time and effort. The procedure is laborious and iterative.

Think about anything you worked hard on for a long time and are now proud of; it may be your fitness or a new language. You'll have some idea of what it's like to practice each day to improve. That's the essence of making money.

His Financial Advice for Individuals in Their Twenties.

The decade of your 20s is a crucial period in your life that poses financial challenges that can be difficult to navigate. As you navigate through life, it is not uncommon to find yourself in a position where you are earning the highest income you have ever received while simultaneously taking on new financial responsibilities.

Moreover, it's likely that you are managing multiple financial aspirations, ranging from contemplating furthering your education to acquiring a residence. You might be experiencing a deficit in terms of initiating your financial journey.

In his book, Ramit Sethi, a self-made millionaire and star of Netflix's "How to Get Rich," shares his best advice for individuals in their 20s regarding money management: setting up an automatic investment.

In one's 20s, it can often seem as though the odds are not in their favor. Perhaps their income is not yet at its peak, they may be grappling with doubts about their chosen profession, and they could be confronted with a daunting pile of student loans. However, the one invaluable asset that they possess is time.

The significance of commencing investments at the earliest possible time cannot be overstated. Investing on a regular basis may appear daunting, particularly if you're struggling to make ends meet. However, Sethi suggests that even a modest, consistent investment can pave the way for a promising tomorrow.

Why It's Smart to Invest While You're Young

The longer you can afford to keep your money invested, the better off you will be. Your investment capital may increase over time thanks to interest, and that growth can be magnified by compound interest.

As one's investment yields returns, the interest accrued not only applies to the initial investment but also to the subsequent returns. The longer you are able to keep your money invested, the greater the potential for growth.

Furthermore, it is worth noting that the stock market does not consistently perform positively. During times of economic recession, it is not uncommon for one's investment portfolio to experience a prolonged period of decline lasting several months or even years.

Throughout history, it has consistently demonstrated resilience and recovered. By investing early, you provide your money with ample time to recuperate from market downturns. By automating your investments, you can cultivate a consistent investing routine.

You may accomplish this either by arranging for payroll deductions at your place of employment or by establishing automated transfers from your bank account to your investment portfolio. For those without an investment account, opening an online brokerage account can be achieved in just a few simple steps.

Retirement accounts such as a 401(k) or an individual retirement account (IRA) are excellent options to consider when planning for retirement. According to Sethi, beginning your financial journey doesn't require a substantial monetary contribution. Initiating the commencement is of utmost significance.

"In one's 20s lies a remarkable opportunity to establish positive habits, regardless of one's income level," he remarks. "As your earnings increase in your 30s and 40s, you can just turn that number up."

Having Fun While You Are Still Young.

Sethi's second piece of advice for those in their twenties is, "Enjoy this season of life." He advises, "Don't try to be 40 before you're 40."

He recommends spending your 20s having fun, meeting new people, and traveling on the cheap.

Accept the fact that you will never again be able to accomplish the things you could in your twenties.

In your twenties, you should focus on establishing a solid financial foundation, but you should also make the most of the boundless enthusiasm, free time, and many chances at your disposal. "That I didn't enjoy myself more is one of my regrets," Sethi admits.

Chapter 9

RAMIT SETHI ON A NETFLIX SHOW

The author, who very much invented the concept of becoming wealthy, is taking his ideas to the small screen. The financial guru and author Ramit Sethi is on the road with a Netflix docuseries based on his New York Times bestseller, "I Will Teach You to Be Rich."

In the program, Sethi travels around the United States for six weeks, offering advice to people in places like New York and California who are having trouble getting their finances under control.

Ramit's method isn't always the same as conventional wisdom. He won't tell you to give up your fancy coffee habit. His advice is to "buy all the latest you want" and to "spend extravagantly on the things you love, as long as you cut costs mercilessly on the things you don't."

He encourages individuals to go forward with expensive life events like weddings and gives them psychological strategies to overcome their reluctance to spend money.

No latest, no vacations, no fun—that's the gist of conventional financial counsel. Ramit Sethi thinks that the key to financial success is accepting a life of plenty.

Sethi told THR in an official statement. The premiere of How to Get Rich on Netflix will allow him to reach a wider audience with his philosophy on how to save more, invest wisely, and enjoy life more freely.

How to Motivate Yourself to Work

"The best money advice I ever got is, ironically, the worst money advice I ever got," shouts Ramit Sethi, 40, a personal finance expert, blogger, and author of the top-selling book I Will Teach You to Be Rich (Workman, 2009). Put a stop to your daily latte habit.

Sethi attempted to save money by forgoing coffee but found it difficult to do so. We overspend just as we overeat, and then we tell ourselves, "Okay, this month I'm going to cut back."

Money is not a matter of willpower, as Sethi has learned from this. Control over one's own behavior is difficult to achieve. We need to put in place structures and programs to ensure the occurrence of desired actions.

By setting up automated contributions for 401(k) plans, student loan repayments, and credit card bills, Sethi encourages his 500,000 online followers in their twenties and thirties to put as much of their financial lives as possible on autopilot. He even devised a plan to coerce himself into going to the fitness center.

When he got out of bed in the morning, his feet accidentally struck his exercise sneakers since he had not placed them near the floor. After he has done that, he will start going to the gym more often.

Don't sweat the small stuff if you want to become wealthy. Rather than worrying about lattes, you should focus on getting five or 10 large successes correctly. Here are three examples: Start saving early, allocate your funds wisely, and negotiate a higher salary.

Learning How to Be Your Own Boss

Join me as we delve into Ramit Sethi's life, where he shares his step-by-step process for building a successful business, sharing your passion with the world, and creating the lifestyle you desire.

Sethi suggests working from home in his book. Perhaps a quaint coffee shop or a cozy corner cafe would be the perfect spot to unwind and recharge during a leisurely 4-week vacation. As time passed, your enterprise flourished and brought forth financial prosperity.

Finding A Job That Pays You More

You should not settle for a job that you despise. It is advisable to always strive for fair compensation that accurately reflects your value. One should not settle for mediocrity and allow their life and career to slip away from them.

In Find Your Dream Job, you will discover the secrets to securing your ideal position at your dream company. This comprehensive guide equips you with effective strategies for navigating tough interview questions and empowers you to negotiate for better compensation and benefits.

Are you prepared to embark on a journey to discover the career of your dreams and receive compensation that truly reflects your value? You should utilize your financial resources to lead a more expansive and fulfilling existence.

For those who have long intended to put their finances in order or are simply prepared to alleviate the associated stress, Sethi offers a direct means of obtaining answers to any monetary inquiries.

Don't hold back on lavishly supporting your passions. Automate your financial life by paying bills, setting money aside for trips and retirement, and so on. And spend it on expanding your horizons and enriching your life.

Chapter 10

PERSONAL LIFE

R amit Singh Sethi, an American author and self-proclaimed expert in personal finance, is known for his work in this field. The esteemed author behind the 2009 New York Times Best Seller, "I Will Teach You to Be Rich," is also the visionary founder of GrowthLab.com, a premier online destination for advertising advice.

Moreover, he is the proprietor and co-originator of PBworks, a for-profit wiki platform.

In the year 2005, a Master of Arts in Sociology (Social Psychology and Interpersonal Processes) was conferred upon him by Stanford. He entered into holy matrimony with Cassandra Campa in the year 2018.

Current Projects

Sethi's website boasts an abundance of complimentary content. Through his series of online courses, he is able to fund his blog almost entirely. The courses delve into topics such as enhancing productivity, refining body language, and discovering one's ideal career.

At times, these highly sought-after items can fetch a price tag exceeding $1,000 and are known to sell out in a flash. In 2015, GrowthLab was launched by Ramit Sethi. The online marketing resource is a valuable tool that assists individuals in launching and expanding their online enterprises.

Similar to Sethi's blog, the majority of GrowthLab's content is offered free of charge, with financial support derived from the online courses.

Where You Can Find Ramit Sethi

Sethi's guidance on achieving financial success can be found on the renowned blog that initiated it all, "I Will Teach You to Be Rich." Therein lies the opportunity to delve deeper into the world of Sethi, peruse his online courses, and acquaint oneself with his various other undertakings. He also has a book out called "I Will Teach You to Be Rich."

Ramit Sethi's YouTube channel is a treasure trove of educational videos and insightful interviews with accomplished individuals. For those who are new to finance, it serves as a great starting point. One may also come across him on Twitter under his handle, @ramit.

Ramit Sethi's Marriage

On the 28th of July, Cassandra Alicia Campa and Ramit Singh Sethi exchanged vows in holy matrimony at the exquisite Ritz-Carlton Lake Tahoe in California. An American Catholic Church pastor by the name of the Reverend Charles Grande presided over the wedding.

Earlier in the day, a Sikh ceremony was conducted by Manjit Singh and Amarjit Singh, both of whom are Sikh priests. At the age of 34, the bride established Next Level Wardrobe, a New York-based company specializing in men's styling.

Upon completing her studies at California State University, Long Beach, she ventured to the University of the Arts, London, to pursue her passion for fashion merchandising. The author is the offspring of Patricia A. Campa and Roy J. Campa, both hailing from Visalia, Calif.

The groom's dad runs a car restoration shop in Visalia called Campa's Custom Painting. Her mom teaches little ones at Linwood Elementary School in Visalia, where she resides.

At the time of their nuptials, the groom was 36 years old and held the esteemed position of founder and chief executive at IWT, a prominent self-development company located in New York.

Additionally, he had authored the widely acclaimed book "I Will Teach You to Be Rich," which offers valuable insights on personal finance. Upon completing his studies at Stanford, he was awarded a master's degree in sociology from the same esteemed institution.

The author is the offspring of Neelam Sethi and Prabhjot S. Sethi, hailing from Sacramento. The mother of the groom concluded her career as an educator at Earl Le Gette Elementary School, situated in Fair Oaks, California. In Sacramento, the father of the groom serves as a mechanical engineer for the California Energy Commission.

In the summer of 2012, fate brought the couple together at a delightful barbecue hosted by a mutual friend in the bustling city of New York.

Chapter 11

30 INSPIRATIONAL RAMIT SETHI QUOTES

1. Treat every whisper from someone you respect like a powerful scream.

2. Seize the moment. Start making your dreams come true today.

3. Success lies not in the abundance of wealth but in the richness of our character.

4. Open your eyes to the abundance of business opportunities surrounding you. Curiosity is the key skill that unlocks the door to entrepreneurial success. Explore new places and perspectives to discover the value of diversity.

5. You are already equipped with everything you need to achieve success. Think highly of yourself and have faith in your skills.

6. Embrace your failures, for they are the stepping stones to success. Strive to fail at least four or five times a month, for it is a sign that you are pushing yourself to your limits.

7. Strive for consistency, but remember that true success requires breaking out of the crowd.

8. Believe in the value of your service and charge accordingly to provide a premium experience.

9. Give back to enrich your life.

10. Embrace your failures, for they hold the key to your success.

11. There are no limits to how much you can earn; there are only limits to how much you can cut.

12. Be more concerned with what you do than what you say. Start making the change you seek. Put your behavior first, and success will follow. Follow your attitude. Embrace the counterintuitive and discover the magic within.

13.   Take action and make the change you need to start your business. Don't let endless blog posts hold you back from achieving your dreams.

14.   The quality of your copywriting determines how others see you. It's not about your products, your customer service, or your academic background.

15.   Words on the page are a canvas for the imagination to paint its masterpiece.

16.   Embrace abundance and take action. If it's on your mind, make it yours. Every second counts; don't waste it on debates. Every idea counts, which makes it all worthwhile.

17.   If it's not meant for you, move on in a world full of endless possibilities.

18.   Don't allow the negativity of critics and naysayers to hinder your pursuit of your dreams. Pay no attention to those who discourage you from enjoying life's simple pleasures, such as lattes and going out.

19. Indulge in the things you love extravagantly while ruthlessly cutting costs on the things you don't. If you can afford it, go for it, whether it's $500 shoes or a luxurious family vacation.

20. If something isn't working, it's time to find a new approach and keep moving forward. Embrace the unknown and dare to do something different.

21. Consider the limitless possibilities of your generosity. Greatness need not come at an exorbitant price.

22. Embrace your current age and enjoy the journey towards 40. Even with just 80 subscribers, every effort towards improvement is worth testing.

23. Remember, 80% of the work is already accomplished before you even enter the room. Embrace a transformative mindset and watch as magical tactics become unnecessary in your pursuit of success.

24.   Success in wealth creation lies not in being the smartest, but in taking the first step towards your goal.

25.   Embrace the challenge of making decisions that lead to a fulfilling life, even if retirement is not an option.

26.   Greatness beckons the busy, inspiring them to mentor.

27.   Those who stick it out to the finish will be rewarded with success. Never let the opinions of self-satisfied individuals who argue over obscure details dim your light. Be the one who takes action and sidesteps the debate.

28.   Embrace your failures, for within them lies precious guidance towards your destined path. Throughout our journey, we have learned to trust the guidance of experts: educators, physicians, and financial advisors.

29.   Remember, expertise is measured by the results you achieve. Your expertise holds true value only when you can deliver what you were hired to do, regardless of your educational background. Choose wisely in life, and you'll never have to fret over saving a few dollars on daily indulgences.

30.   Choose to invest extravagantly in the things you love and ruthlessly cut costs on the things you don't.

Printed in Great Britain
by Amazon

25408989R00051